OLD ROSES

Published by Grange Books
An imprint of Grange Books Limited
The Grange
Grange Yard
London SE1 3AG

ISBN 1 85627 360 1

Reprinted 1993

First published by Webb & Bower
(Publishers) Limited 1983

Printed and bound in Singapore.

OLD ROSES

Lesley Gordon

Grange BOOKS

Rosa Pumila

Rosa gallica pumila

It is fortunate that Redouté has left us this portrait of *R.gallica pumila*, which he calls the Rose of Love, since it has become a rare collectors' flower. It is to this Raphael of flowers as Redouté was called, that we owe as much as we do about roses that have disappeared or are endangered.

Pierre-Joseph Redouté was born on 10 July 1759 at St Hubert, near Namur. As an already talented boy, he was sent to the Abbey of Orval, which had an excellent reputation for teaching arts and crafts. In his early years he began portrait painting, then went to Paris to continue his studies where he met L'Héritier, who first aroused his interest in flowers. He passed on to Gerard von Spaëndonck who was his next master. In 1788, Redouté visited England with L'Héritier, in order to learn new methods of colour printing, in particular, stipple engraving.

Back in France, Louis XV was his first great patron, and Marie Antoinette appointed him her *Peintre du Cabinet*. He survived the Revolution and was made Flower Painter to the Nation. Josephine Bonaparte made him her Court Painter and commissioned him to paint 250 species of roses in her garden at Malmaison.

While he was examining a white lily, Redouté suffered a stroke, and died the next day, 19 July 1840.

Recipe for Content

To quit his care, he gathered, first of all
In spring the Roses, Apples in the fall   *Virgil, c.37 BC*

Rosa Pumila.   *Rosier d'Amour.*

Agatha Incarnate

Rosa agathe incarnata

The Agatha rose is dedicated to a Christian martyr, St Agatha, a Sicilian virgin, born at Palermo, and put to death by Quintianus, Governor of Sicily in AD 251, because she rejected his advances. Her feast day is 5 February and she has, not a rose, but a primrose for her flower.

The Agatha rose is, or was, a large flowered rose, known in Provence about 1435. For a virgin saint, she has a remarkable number of varieties named in her honour: Admirable Agatha, Beautiful Iris Agatha, Beloved Agatha, Agatha of the King, Agatha Triumph of Venus—surely a remarkable marriage of Christian and pagan—Agatha Great Sultana, Agatha Supreme and Voluptuous Agatha. It would seem that the French rose growers of that period before the Revolution became a little confused in their nomenclature.

Few may remain of that prolific family, but Edward Bunyard mentioned the 'Agathes' as smaller editions of the cabbage rose, so she is not entirely forgotten. The Agatha incarnata, known to Philip Miller as *Rosa incarnata*, is neat, tidy and very sweetly scented, and seems to be the sole survivor of the charming and numerous family.

For Mankind's Ailments

No man can say, no man remember, How many uses there are
For Oil of Roses as a cure for mankind's ailments.

Walafrid Strabo, c.842

ROSA *incarnata* Park Floral

Maxima

Rosa gallica officinalis

This ageless rose of many names is thought to be the once 'red damask' and it was the one most often used as the apothecary rose. It is also likely to have been the rose that Edmund of Lancaster brought from Provins in 1279 to become the Red rose of Lancaster.

Its ancient history may perhaps start with such a rose pictured in a Minoan fresco dated at between 1500 and 1600 BC, which is believed to have been the gallica rose. Its modern chapter takes us to the Crusades, and the rose that was taken to Provins by the Crusaders. This rose, that found its way to England in the thirteenth century, closely resembled *R.gallica officinalis*, previously known as Maxima, probably the oldest cultivated form of *R.gallica*.

The late eighteenth century is the classical period of the gallica rose, but only a few of the roses that Redouté knew and grew are still listed today. Now *officinalis* and *versicolor* mingle neatly as hedge roses, still regarded with interest as something rather 'old world', or seen by others as something new and smart, and the gallica's bright red continues to run in the petals of today's red rose.

Confectio Rosae Gallicae

Fresh red rose petals	250 grammes
Refined sugar	750 grammes
Beat together in a stone mortar	

Avicenna, eleventh century AD

Rosa Gallica officinalis.   *Rosier de Provins ordinaire.*

Rosa Mundi

Rosa gallica versicolor

The striped form of the province rose, *R. gallica versicolor*, was once the heroine of a romantic story. She was said to have taken her name from Fair Rosamond—Rosamond de Clifford, the mistress of Henry II, who died at Woodstock in 1176, having been poisoned by Henry's Queen, Eleanor of Aquitaine, in a fit of jealous rage.

The late Norman Young, in his book, *The Complete Rosarian*, has ruthlessly shattered Fair Rosamond's romance as regards her connection with the rose, and gives dates to prove his case. He clinches the argument by quoting from the *Garden Book* of Sir Thomas Hanmer, written in 1659. 'Rosa Mundi' [Hanmer also calls it the Christmas rose], 'another new stript or variegated rose, first found in Norfolke a few years since, upon a branch of the common Red Rose, and from thence multiplied. It is like the Red in all things' [thus allying it with the gallicas] 'but that it is stript in great flakes with indifferent White.'

Luckily for her, this lovely flower has an unforgettable name of her own, Rosa Mundi, the Rose of all the World.

Milk of Roses

Ladies may make their own milk of roses, by simply adding one ounce of the oil of almonds to a pint of rose water, after which ten drops of the oil of tartar is to be added.

Henry Phillips, 1780–1832

Rosa Mundi

La Belle Sultane

Rosa gallica violacea

These are a leggy group centering around *Gallica violacea*, appearing a good deal later than *R.gallica officinalis*. They are closely connected with the velvet roses.

They grow in clusters six to eight feet high, and appear to be a different development of the gallicas, with possibly a damask inheritance, and derived from some specialized condition or with a hybrid strain about them. The stems are set with reddish bristles, and the flowers are composed of two layers of petals, deep crimson and suffused with purple, having an almost white central zone surrounding a centre of golden stamens. With age the flower changes to violet crimson declining into slate or a violet-brown. With this sad departure of youth, the stamens blacken. It has an early but short blooming season. According to Graham Thomas, it is a difficult rose to place, both in a book and in a garden.

Waste Not, Want Not

The nailes or white ends of the leaves of the floures are good for watering eies.

Gerard, 1545–1612

Rosa Gallica Maheka. (flore subsimplici). *Le Maheka à fleurs simples.*

13

Celsiana

Rosa damascena celsiana

The origin of the damask rose, *R.damascena*, is obscure, although Hakluyt writes in 1582 that 'in time of memory many things have been brought in that were not here before, as the Damaske Rose by Doctour Linaker, King Henry the Seventh and King Henrie the Eight's Physician'. The Elizabethans frequently made use of damask rose petals, but we have no firm knowledge of its earlier history, though it seems probable that it was brought to Europe from the East by the Crusaders. Kinglake in *Eothen*, 1844, describes the roses growing in Damascus to an immense height and size, and profusion, and loading 'the slow aire with their damask breath'.

Redouté painted seven varieties of the damask rose, although nine were listed as growing at Malmaison. Celsiana received its name from Cels, a Parisian nurseryman, who introduced it into France.

Although damask roses were grown in Persia, Turkey, Bulgaria and in India for the distilling of attar of roses, yet Sir Francis Bacon said of them that 'Roses, damask and red, are fast flowers of their smells; so that you may walk by a whole row of them, and find nothing of their sweetness; yea, though it be in a morning's dew'.

In the Kitchen
Cookes and gentlewomen do make rose tartes
and such like dishes.

Anon.

Rosa Damascena.   *Rosier de Cels.*

The York and Lancaster Rose

Rosa damascena versicolor

We may believe in the York and Lancaster rose, *R. versicolor*, indeed we must, for we still grow it in our gardens; but we must no longer believe that splendid quarrel scene between Richard Plantagenet and the Earl of Somerset in the Temple Garden in Henry VI part 1, when red roses and white were torn from their bushes to serve as badges for the opposing armies of Lancaster and York. That, we are told, may be Shakespeare, but it is not history.

According to Norman Young, the White rose was the Yorkist badge fifty years before that scene, and the Red rose of Lancaster was older still by a hundred years. But after the Wars of the Roses ended, the Red rose of Lancaster and the White rose of York were finally combined in the symbolic red and white Tudor rose.

R. damascena versicolor, with its blush-white and pale pink flowers, lacks the firm stripes of Rosa Mundi. But it has a sweet scent and a name given as a symbol of peace.

York and Lancaster

If this pale rose offend your sight,
It in your bosom wear;
'Twill blush to find itself less white,
And turn Lancastrian there.

William Somerville 1675–1742

The York and Lancaster Rose.

Autumn Damask

Rosa damascena bifera

The Autumn Damask, here painted by Mary Lawrance, was called by the ancients Rosa Bifera, the Biflorus Rose, and by the moderns, Rose de Quatre Saisons or the Rose of Every Month. Before 1800, this was the only rose that bloomed more than once a year; that is, in June and July.

R. bifera was the result of a union between *R. gallica* and *R. moschata*, and Redouté knew it as Rosier des Parfumeurs. It was cultivated up to the First Empire on Mount Valérien, near Paris, opposite Bagatelle, which had not then its famous Rosary. The roses were used in the making of pharmaceutical rose water and essence of roses.

Sir Thomas Hanmer gives the first mention of the Autumn Damask in England. '*The Monthly Rose*, a very Damaske in leaves and sent, but it beares two or three moneths more in the yeare than the ordinary Damaske, and very plentifully, if it stand warme. It is called often Rosa Italica.'

The Man Who Invented Cold Cream

Galen's rose oil was not the otto of rose we now call oil of rose, but ordinary olive oil in which twelve ounces of rose buds had been macerated in relays of four ounces each

Galen, Physician to Marcus Aurelius,
second century AD

Rosa damascena d.   Red Monthly Rose

The Celestial Rose

Rosa alba celeste

The story of the white rose goes back to Saxon days in England, and it can be traced through the civilizations of Europe more certainly than any other cultivated rose.

Rosa alba is probably a hybrid of *R.damascena* and *R.canina*, and can be confusing because it may be white, but more often it is pink. Although it has a fragility and delicacy suggestive of the silken decor of the boudoir, it is actually hardy, vigorous and content under all conditions.

Celeste, the Celestial rose, is here pictured by Redouté under the name of *R.damascena*, 'Aurora', 'Le Rosier Aurore Poniatowska', and he places it among the damasks, which is another confusion typical in the life of the albas. Celeste makes a four-foot bush, with shell-pink roses that are semi-double, set among steely-grey leaves, the stems furnished with a few thin red thorns. Vita Sackville-West describes this rose as 'one of the loveliest shrubs one could ever wish to contemplate'.

For the Town-dweller

Who, that hath reason and his Smell
Would not among roses and Jasmine dwell,
    Rather than all his Spirits choak
With exhalations of Durt and Smoak,
      And all th'uncleanness which does drown
In Pestilential Clouds a populous Town?

Abraham Cowley, 1668

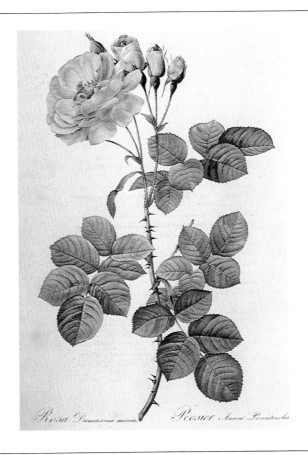

Rosa Damascena aurea. *Rosier Aurore Poniatowska.*

The Great Maiden's Blush

Rosa alba regalis

The story, indeed the scandal, of the Great Maiden's Blush, is rare in rose history. Known to Redouté when he painted her as *R. alba regalis*, the Regal Rose, or perhaps La Royale, as she also became, seems to suggest an aloofness consistent with La Virginale, another name bestowed on her. And then we have Incarnata! Why, or perhaps how, did this rose acquire the name of La Séduisante, and what is more—Cuisse de Nymphe, a nymph's thigh? Vita Sackville-West noted that 'the Maiden's Blush holds her petals longer than most', but did she hold them long enough? It would seem that the Cuisse de Nymphe is best forgotten and her story repeated only, as they say, *sub rosa*.

Softly pink and sweetly scented, blooming serenely amongst her grey-green foliage, she is obviously a treasure, and unlike more worldly treasures, she requires no special care. The flowering shoots grow few or no thorns, but the stout branches that come with middle age, bear large and spiteful thorns.

Gather Ye Roses

For if I wait, said she,
Till time for roses be,
For the moss rose and the musk rose,
Maiden blush and royal disk rose,
What Glory this for me
In such a company.

E.B. Browning, 1806–81

Rosa alba Regalis.

Rosier blanc Royal.

The Great Double White

Rosa alba maxima

The great double white rose, the Jacobite rose, is closely related to the Maiden's Blush, but with creamy white petals, doubled and blush-centred. The blush disappears with age, and the flower becomes completely white. Once blooming, the shrub combines the albas' look of delicacy with extreme toughness, and it will produce a show of bloom under the poorest conditions. The blooms are followed by hips, an attractive sight among the grey-green leaves. It grows to between six and eight feet. This splendid rose is probably a cross between *R.damascena* and *R.canina*.

The species dates back to the Middle Ages, and already in 1307 this rose was being recommended for use as a hedge. This is the double white rose that is to be seen in most of the old flower paintings.

The white Jacobite rose was chosen to celebrate the birth of the Old Pretender, James Francis Edward on 10 June 1688. James's son, Charles Edward, the Young Pretender, Bonnie Prince Charlie to his adherents, took over the Jacobite rose and it flourished in many a Scottish garden, and spoke silently of loyalty to the Jacobite cause.

Birthday Song of the Old Pretender

Of all the days that's in the year
The tenth of June I love most dear,
When sweet white roses do appear,
For the sake of James the rover.

Anon.

Pl. 25

Rosa alba β

Double White Rose

The White Rose of York

Rosa alba semi-plena

A semi-double rose, high-lighted with golden stamens, one of the loveliest in growth, the White rose of York sprays its milk-white clusters over the crumpled grey-green foliage of its kind. It has a rich fragrance which later gives way to a splendid crop of red hips.

Graham Thomas suggests that *R. alba* may be one of the roses planted as a hedge around the fields of damask roses in Bulgaria, grown for distilling attar. Being taller and hardier than the damasks, it helps to shelter them from the icy winds that blow down from the mountains in winter. The quality of the attar of the albas being reduced, it fetches a lower price than that of the damasks.

Writing in 1896, Dean Hole seems to have taken an unnecessarily resigned view of the fate of both the albas and the gallicas, for both now seem to be growing from strength to strength, and interest in many types of shrub roses is increasing. 'The Albas and the Gallicas have almost vanished from our gardens,' he says, 'nor do I plead for their restoration, because, beautiful as they were, we have gained from the development of selection and culture more charming roses in their place.'

The Cosmetic Rose

The petals are burned to make an ingredient of cosmetics for the eyebrows and dried rose leaves are sprinkled on [chafed] thighs.

Pliny, first century AD

Rosa alba flore pleno.   *Rosier blanc ordinaire.*

The Cabbage Rose

Rosa centifolia foliacea

In the past it was believed that the scented rose of Herodotus, actually named by Theophrastus and Pliny as *Rosa centifolia* was the ancestor of our Cabbage rose. Today, following the researches of Bunyard and more recently, Graham Thomas, it has been shown that our rose is not a wild species, but a complex hybrid of four different species, *R. rubra*, *R. phoenicia*, *R. moschata* and *R. canina*. The Dutch breeders slowly and skilfully developed this rose between 1580 and 1710 and Robert Furber illustrated it in his calendar for June, as the 'Dutch hundred leav'd Rose'.

Indeed, the rose, painted here by Georg Ehret, has a singularly Dutch appearance, and Bunyard says that centifolias have a well-fed Dutch bourgeois look, 'a Franz Hals to the Damask's Fragonard'. It has yet to live down its name of cabbage, although *chou*, we understand, is a term of endearment to the French.

Thoughts from Sissinghurst

The scent of the Musk and Damask and Cabbage is unequalled; the charm of the flower is subtle and recalls old needlework and Dutch flower paintings; what more could be asked of any flower.

V. Sackville-West, 1968

The Dutch hundred-leaved Rose.

The Lettuce-Leaved Rose

Rosa centifolia bullata

Said to have been a novelty from Holland, this many-petalled fragrant rose was once in almost every garden. The leaves from which it gets the name of the Lettuce-Leaved rose are strange indeed, and have given rise to much difference of opinion, from Bunyard's, 'not of any beauty, the leaves looking too coarse and Savoy-like', to Graham Thomas's, 'the leaves are remarkable and are in their way the most handsome in the genus'. The leaflets are curiously large and lax, hanging loosely from their stalks, and turning from bronze to mahogany during the course of the summer. The flowers are a pure soft pink, sweetly scented and recurrent. The shrub grows to about four feet by four feet.

Rose Water

Gather two pounds of scented rose petals and add water, preferably rain-water, to just cover. Bring slowly to the boil and simmer for a few minutes. Very fragrant to wash in, and a pleasant welcome for a guest arriving from a distance.

Anon.

Rosa centifolia Bullata
Rosier à feuilles de Laitue

Rose de Meaux

Rosa centifolia pomponia

Gallicas, centifolias, damasks and chinas have all at some time given miniature forms, which were at first called pompons. The Centifolia de Meaux illustrated here by Mary Lawrance would have been very sweetly scented, according to Bunyard. Present varieties are less so. This is a diminutive form of the Cabbage rose, named after Domenique Séguir, Bishop of Meaux, in 1637, who was a patron of horticulture and in particular a lover of roses.

Rose de Meaux is an irresistible small bush, eighteen inches to three feet high, with grey-green foliage and clusters of double roses, each with outer petals of pale pink, deepening in colour at the centre. These little roses are rather pomponia than centifolia, that is, they open flat from their perfect buds, and are not cabbage-shaped. The stems are green, turning to red, and the leaflets downy beneath, with a few thorns mid-rib. They require pruning after flowering to get fresh wood each year.

In the Herb Garden

Who is going to make a pound of pot-pourri [worth having] out of a whole tentful of fashionable Roses? In the Herb garden we would have the Moss Rose, the Damask Rose and the Cabbage Rose. The Cabbage Rose makes the best rose-water, and the Wild Briar or Dog Rose, is one of the most valuable for its curative qualities.

Frances A. Bardswell, 1930

Rosa provincialis E.
ou Rose de meaux.

The Burgundy Rose

Rosa parvifolia

This charming little plum-coloured rose with compact and upright habit, is stated by Bunyard to be a gallica of considerable antiquity. It is small, but not miniature, and dates from its appearance in 1664 in a book by Tabernaemontanus. The Burgundy rose is densely covered with dark grey-green leaves, and its tight rosette flowers are rosy claret or plum, with paler centres.

John Lindley, however, considered the little rose to be distinct from gallica and made it a species, which he called *Rosa parvifolia*. This variety is said to have been found growing wild in a hill near Dijon.

Mary Lawrance, the artist here, was the first woman to publish her flower paintings. *The Various Kinds of Roses cultivated in England*, published in 1799, were drawn and painted from nature with great softness and delicacy. She published her *Sketches of Flowers from Nature* in 1801, and a work on passion flowers in 1802. She was a teacher of botanical drawing and produced thirty-nine coloured plates of roses in all.

The Useful Rose

The distilled water of Roses is good for the strengthening of the heart, and refreshing of the spirits, and likewise for all things that require a gentle cooling. The same being put in junketting dishes, cakes, sauces, and many other pleasant things, giveth a fine and delectable taste.

Gerard, 1545–1612

Rosa centifolia
Burgundy Rose

The Village Maid

Rosa centifolia variegata

This centifolia variety, Village Maid, is also known as Belle des Jardins and Rubannée, the ribboned or striped rose. It is a unique shrub, producing blooms of white striped with lilac, vigorous and thorny, of recurring habit, about six by four feet. The leaves are rough and coarsely toothed.

Discussing the tall stout Village Maid, and wondering how she would appear to us when wind and rain had deprived her of her lilac-ribboned charm, brings to mind Dean Hole, when he tired of the perpetual damasks. 'A tender sadness comes to me thus speaking of them, a melancholy regret, as when one meets in mid-life some goddess of our early youth, and, out upon Time! she has no more figure that a lighthouse, and almost as much crimson in her glowing countenance as there is in its revolving light', and we are as surprised and disappointed as was Charles Kirkpatrick Sharpe, when he met Mrs Siddons at Abbotsford, and 'she ate boiled beef and swilled porter and took snuff and laughed till she made the whole room shake'. 'I do not mean that these Perpetual Damasks are too robust and ruddy', went on the Dean plaintively, 'but they charm us no more.'

A Thorny Question

Bush, why dost bear a rose? If none must have it,
Why dost expose it, yet claw those that crave?

John Bunyan, c.1684

Rosa Centifolia mutabilis.   *Rosier unique.*

The Moss Rose

Rosa centifolia muscosa

No one has yet discovered exactly when and why the first Cabbage rose modestly clothed itself in moss. We know that it was grown in the Botanical Gardens in Leiden in 1720, and we know that it made its first public appearance in England in Robert Furber's catalogue of 1727.

Few flower lovers can withstand the appeal of those cosy little buds, and our grandmothers and great-grandmothers received them on valentines, pasted their pictures into scrapbooks, painted them in watercolours, and embroidered them with coloured silks and Berlin wools, with varying degrees of skill.

Charming as it is, it has some drawbacks of which a short blooming season is one, although some varieties have a second flowering period. It is also subject to mildew, and a combination of moss and mildew can be a sorry sight.

A Moss rose of tremendous character is William Lobb, 1855, named after the gardener and plant-hunter who, according to Tyler Whittle, risked his personal safety to the point of lunacy. What more splendid memorial can William Lobb have been given than these beautiful mossy roses, changing from lilac-rose to slate-blue.

For the Vicar's Garden Party

Use freshly gathered red or pink sweet-scented petals. Cut the bread and butter thinly, and place the petals between the slices, and cut off the crusts. Decorate the serving plate with rose petals.

Anon.

Rosa muscosa   *Moss Provence Rose*

The White Moss Rose

Rosa centifolia muscosa alba

The White Moss rose appeared as a variation of the old Moss rose in 1735, and the Striped Moss rose as a sport of the White Moss rose in 1790. Its story is one of increasing variety, but all within the original species.

When William Paul, the rose specialist, published in his book, *The Rose Garden*, a list showing the decline in popularity of the old Moss roses, *Centifolia muscosa* fared better than most. Sadly, although there are several White Moss roses still in cultivation, they are all susceptible to rain damage, and are usually avoided.

This is a vigorous shrub or semi-climber, of importance if only because of its parenthood to many of the lovely hybrid musks so valuable in the garden. Large clusters of creamy white flowers are produced in late summer. It is a recurrent rose which can reach ten by ten feet.

Receipt for an Impecunious Artist

The white leaves [of roses] stamped in a wooden dish with
a piece of Allum and the juyce strained forth into some
glass vessel, dried in the shadow, and kept, is the most fine
and pleasant yellow colour that may be devised . . . to limne
or wash pictures and Imagerie in books.

Gerard, 1545–1612

Rosa Muscosa alba.   *Rosier Mousseux à fleurs blanches.*

The Monthly Rose

Rosa chinensis semperflorens

This lovely rose, also known as the Blush Monthly, may have been introduced by Sir Joseph Banks in 1789, but claims are contradictory and all that is certain is that the china roses, so ancient in the East, made a most definite forward step in western rose cultivation when, as Vita Sackville-West said, 'China opened her shut gate to let her roses through'.

In 1823 Henry Phillips in *Sylva Florifera*, describes how on its arrival in England it was considered to be so delicate that 'it was kept constantly in the stove, and the smallest cuttings were sold for many guineas each'. Soon it was found so easy to propagate that 'every country casement had the pride of sheltering this Chinese prodigy, until the cottager, for want of pence to purchase flower pots, planted it in the open ground, where it blooms happily throughout the summer and may often be seen, "its petals pushing through a veil of snow in the month of December"'.

Art, Science and the Rose

You see, sweet maid, we marry
A gentler scion to the wildest stock,
And make conceive a bark of baser kind
By bud of nobler race: this is art
Which does mend nature, change it rather, but
The art itself is nature.

William Shakespeare, 1564–1616

Copper Austrian Briar

Rosa foetida bicolor

This is an old briar rose, cultivated before 1590, and the source of much of the flamboyance in the roses of today. Even its name is a warning, *R. foetida*, which is a rather sharp reference to its heavy scent. In the rose-garden, scarcely any other rose would welcome its company either, only the yellows could be comfortable. It needs the setting of a shrubbery, or a tall hedge in full sun as a background to its coppery-red blooms. Bunyard describes them as nasturtium scarlet, and in France they are known as *capucine* meaning nasturtium, or *ponceau*, from the corn poppy. Being a sport of the pure yellow *R. foetida lutea*, it adds to its colourful confusion by occasionally reverting to yellow and surprising us by producing both yellow and copper-red on the same branch, or two-coloured flowers or even bi-coloured petals.

Alfred Parsons, the painter of this rose, was born in 1847, and died in 1920. He was well-known first as a landscape artist, but later worked on a large number of black and white drawings for William Robinson's *The English Flower Garden* and *The Wild Garden*. His greatest opportunity came when he painted his colour illustrations for Ellen Willmott's *The Genus Rosa*.

Common or Garden

Any nose
May ravage with impunity a rose.

Robert Browning, 1855

The Royal Virgin Rose Without Thorns

Rosa pendulina, Rosa alpina

This graceful red rose is the wild alpine rose of the mountains of central and southern Europe. It was illustrated in Besler's *Hortus Eystettensio*, 1613, under the name of *Rosa rubra praecox*, but it does not seem to have reached England until James Sutherland, later King's Botanist to William III introduced it in 1683. The name *R.pendulina* refers to the hanging fruit.

Georg Ehret, the artist here, was born in Heidelberg in 1708 of humble parents who earned a living selling garden produce. His father died, and his mother married the head-gardener of the Elector of Heidelberg, and young Georg had partial charge of one of the two gardens. After travelling in France and Holland, he finally settled in England, where he was made a Fellow of the Royal Society in 1757. He died in 1770.

For the Stillroom

Of the Red Roses are usually made many compositions;
viz, Electuary of Roses . . . Sugar of Roses, Oyntment and
Oyl of Roses. . . . To write at large of every one of these,
would make my Book smell too big.

Nicholas Culpeper, 1653

The Royal Virgin Rose without Thorns.

Sources and Acknowledgements

Georg Dionysius Ehret, watercolours (Victoria and Albert Museum): p. 7, 11, 17, 29, 47

Mary Lawrance, *Various Kinds of Roses Cultivated in Britain*, 1799, title page, p. 19, 25, 33, 35, 39

Alfred Parsons, watercolours for Ellen Wilmot, *The Genus Rosa*, 1910–1914 (Lindley Library): p. 43, 45

Pierre-Joseph Redouté, *Les Roses*, 1817–1824: p. 5, 9, 13, 15, 21, 23, 27, 31, 37, 41

The photographs were taken by Eileen Tweedy.

The publishers would like to thank the staff of the library of the Royal Botanic Gardens, Kew for their help in producing this book.